HAL LEONARD LOOG GUITAR METHOD

DAVID D. MILLS

Video Performance and Production: Doug Boduch
Vocals: Sarah LeMieux

To access video visit:
www.halleonard.com/mylibrary

Enter Code
5726-6665-4756-0020

ISBN 978-1-70510-338-8

Visit Hal Leonard Online at
www.halleonard.com

Contact us:
Hal Leonard
7777 West Bluemound Road
Milwaukee, WI 53213
Email: info@halleonard.com

In Europe, contact:
Hal Leonard Europe Limited
42 Wigmore Street
Marylebone, London, W1U 2RN
Email: info@halleonardeurope.com

In Australia, contact:
Hal Leonard Australia Pty. Ltd.
4 Lentara Court
Cheltenham, Victoria, 3192 Australia
Email: info@halleonard.com.au

INTRODUCTION

Welcome to the *Hal Leonard Loog Guitar Method*! The Loog guitar is a fun, easy-to-learn instrument for all ages, and also serves as a perfect introduction to standard guitar. This beginner's method teaches the basics of the three-string Loog guitar from the ground up—with chords, strumming techniques, fun songs, and much more. Soon you'll be strumming, picking, and singing your favorite songs!

VIDEOS

The videos that accompany this book feature a Loog Pro Acoustic guitar. Access the videos for download or streaming by visiting *www.halleonard.com/mylibrary* and entering the code from page 1 of this book. Examples demonstrated on video are marked in the book with this symbol: ▶

PARTS OF THE LOOG GUITAR

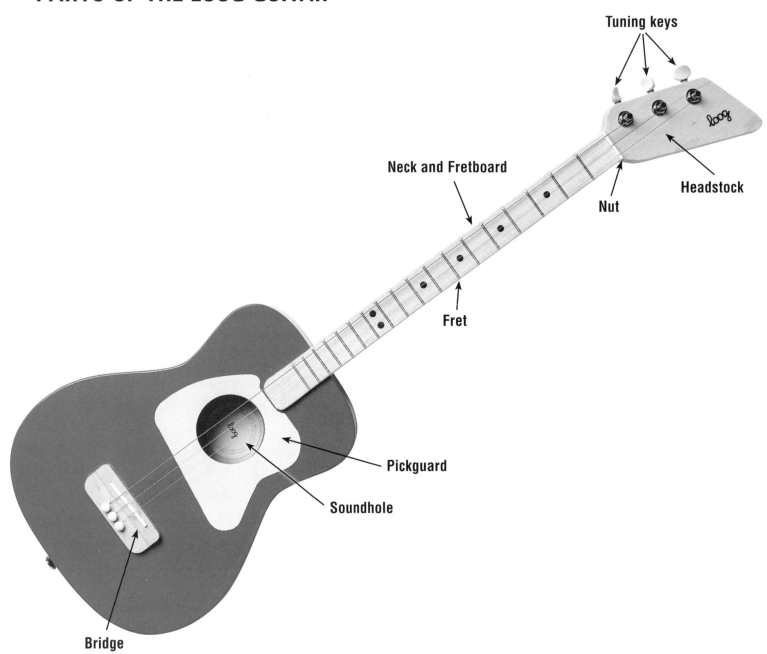

Tuning keys

Neck and Fretboard

Headstock

Nut

Fret

Pickguard

Soundhole

Bridge

PLAYING POSITION

Adjust your strap to a length that allows you to set the Loog guitar on your leg when sitting down. That way the guitar will be in the same position when you are standing up.

The Loog has a relatively long neck for a lightweight guitar. If you brace the body of the guitar with your strumming arm, the neck will not droop down; you do not want to be holding up the neck with your fretting fingers. (Note: If you're an adult, you can hold the Loog guitar against your body like a ukulele.)

Place only your thumb on the back of the neck so you can move your hand quickly and easily. Avoid squeezing the neck with the palm of your hand.

Fretting-hand fingers are numbered 1 through 4. (Pianists: Note that the thumb is *not* number 1.)

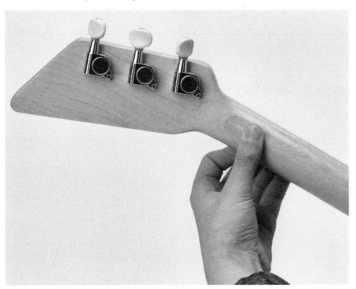 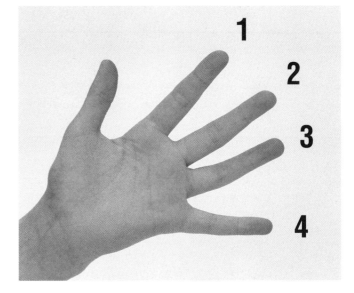

HOLDING THE PICK

This photo shows how to hold the pick in your strumming hand. You should maintain a loose wrist for strumming. Your forearm should remain against the edge of the guitar as shown on the previous page.

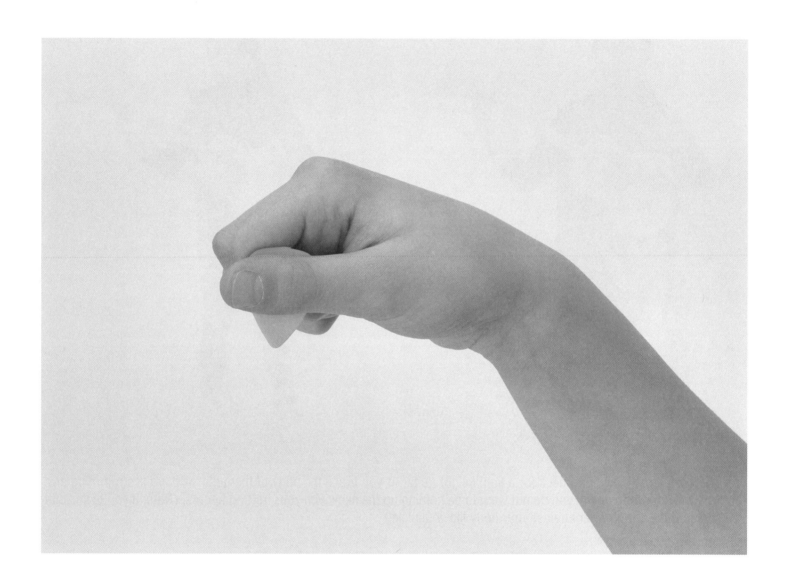

To get used to holding the pick, try strumming down repeatedly across the strings with no fingers on the fretboard.

TUNING

The most efficient way to tune the Loog guitar is to invest in a clip-on headstock tuner. Many tuners work with various instruments, so set the tuner on "guitar" and "440" for standard pitch. The Loog guitar strings are G–B–E, with E being the highest-pitched string and the closest to the floor (exactly the same as the first three strings of a standard guitar). When you pluck each individual string, the headstock tuner will identify the pitch. Turn the corresponding tuning key until the headstock tuner indicates the string is neither *sharp* (too high) nor *flat* (too low). Most headstock tuners light up green when the string is in tune.

If you want to tune to a keyboard, press down the appropriate key on the piano and turn the tuning keys on the guitar until you match the pitch.

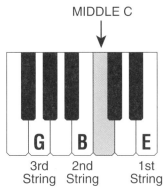

You can also take advantage of the free Loog Guitar app, which includes an easy-to-use tuner as well as many other helpful features.

RELATIVE TUNING

If you don't have access to a tuner, you can make sure the guitar is in tune with itself using *relative tuning*. You'll need to get more familiar with the Loog and the notes on the fretboard first, but the process is quick and easy:

1. First, play a B on the G string and match its tone to the sound of the open B string by adjusting the tuning key.

2. Then, play an E on the B string and match it to the open E string.

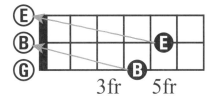

THE C CHORD

READING CHORD DIAGRAMS

In this book, you will be strumming *chords*, which consist of three notes played at the same time. *Chord diagrams* show you the fingerings for chords.

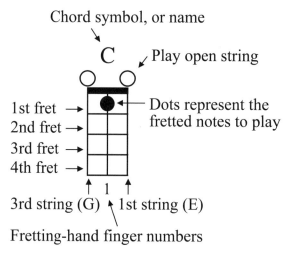

It's time to learn your first chord! The C chord is played by curving the 1st finger of your left hand over the 1st string (the E string) and pressing your fingertip down just behind the 1st fret of the 2nd string (the B string). With your pick, strum downward across all three strings in one motion.

Check that all three strings are ringing by picking each string individually to make sure you are not touching the open E or open G strings with your finger, which would stop them from ringing out.

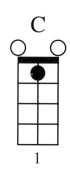

Let's try out your first chord with a simple strum exercise. Strum down once for each slash mark. Start by counting "1, 2, 3, 4" in a slow, steady pulse. Keep counting the same way as you play through it.

C Chord Strum

C

/	/	/	/		/	/	/	/
Count: 1 2 3 4   1 2 3 4

/	/	/	/		/	/	/	/
1 2 3 4   1 2 3 4

READ AND PLAY

THE STAFF

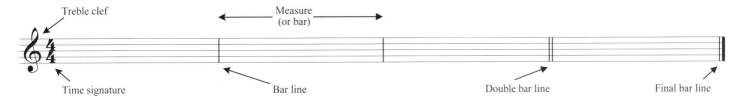

What you see above is a music *staff*. *Bar lines* divide the staff into *measures*, or *bars*. The symbol at the beginning of the staff is the *treble clef*. The 4/4 is a *time signature* that tells us there are four beats in each measure. A *double bar line* marks the end of a section or short example, and a *final bar line* marks the end of a song.

Each line and space of the staff has a letter name. The lines from bottom to top are E–G–B–D–F. The spaces from bottom to top are F–A–C–E. Because there are only three strings on the Loog, the notes we're mostly concerned with are G–B–D–F on the lines and A–C–E on the spaces.

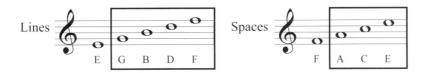

NOTE AND REST VALUES

The notes in the staff above are: a *whole note* lasting four beats, *half notes* lasting two beats each, *quarter notes* lasting one beat each, and *eighth notes* lasting one-half beat each. The last measure has a combination of quarter notes and eighth notes to show that two eighth notes are equal to one quarter note.

RHYTHMIC NOTATION

The example above shows *rhythmic notation*, which tells you the duration of each chord, or how long each chord is supposed to ring out before playing the next one. In the third measure are *slashes*—one for each beat; you can strum your own rhythm over that space of time.

Let's take a Rhythm Ride! While fretting your C chord, strum down across the strings on each note, and miss the strings when bringing your hand back up. For a whole note or half note, you will continue this strumming motion on every beat but hit the strings only on the first downward motion. Count along as you play.

Rhythm Ride

REST VALUES

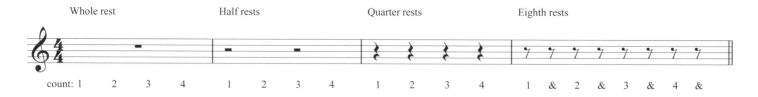

The symbols in the staff above are *rests*, or periods of silence. From left to right, they are: a *whole rest* lasting four beats, *half rests* lasting two beats each, *quarter rests* lasting one beat each, and *eighth rests* lasting one-half beat each.

In the next exercise, play a C chord and use all downstrums for the notes again. For the rests, you'll need to stop the strings from ringing by laying your pick-hand palm across them. You can also release the pressure of your fretting-hand finger(s) to help mute the sound during the rests.

There are lyrics below each line. Speak the words as you strum; this will help you get a feel for the rhythm.

Play and Rest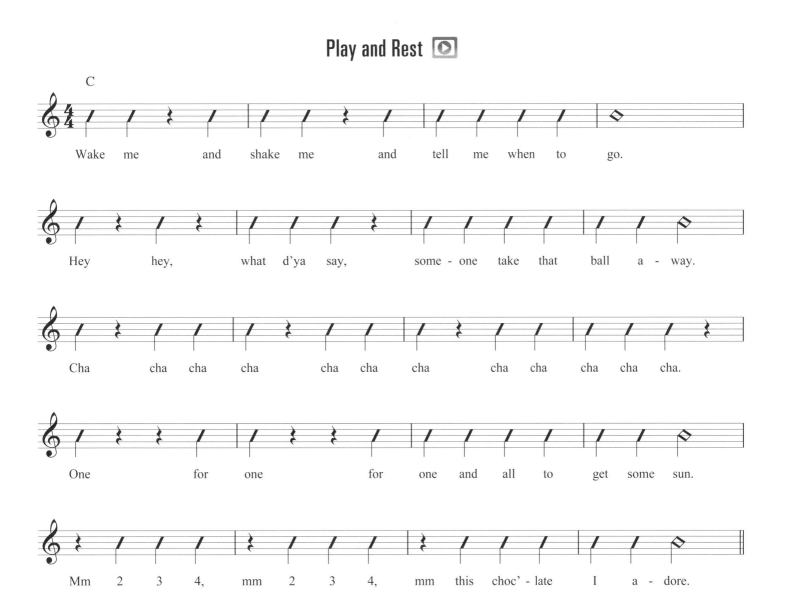

REPEATS

In the example below, the two measures are bracketed by *repeat signs*, which tell you to repeat what is between those two markings. Repeat signs are very common in music; in fact, you're sure to see some in this book!

THE G CHORD

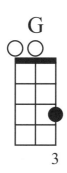

To play the G chord, hold down the 3rd fret of the 1st string (the E string) with your 3rd finger, then strum down across all the strings at once. Get acquainted with the G chord by playing the following quick exercise:

G Chord Strum ▶

CHANGING CHORDS

Now that you've learned two chords, it's time to practice switching between them. As you play through the following exercise, focus on keeping a steady rhythm while you switch between the C and G chords. Don't slow down when it's time to change your fretting-hand fingers—keep it smooth!

Keep It Smooth! ▶

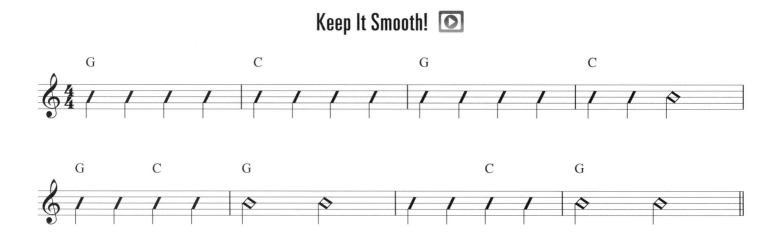

Let's get used to changing chords by strumming through some familiar songs. Use downstrums throughout and sing along while you play—you probably know the lyrics! Also, notice the repeat signs. When you reach the end of the song, the repeat sign tells you to go back to the start without missing a beat and continue playing all the way through the song again.

Row, Row, Row Your Boat

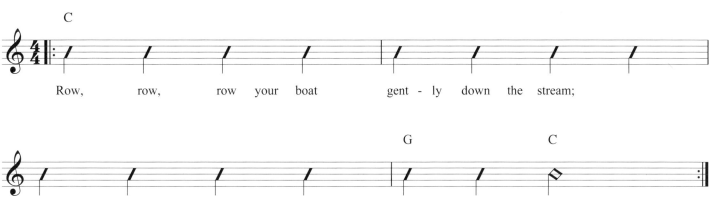

Three Blind Mice

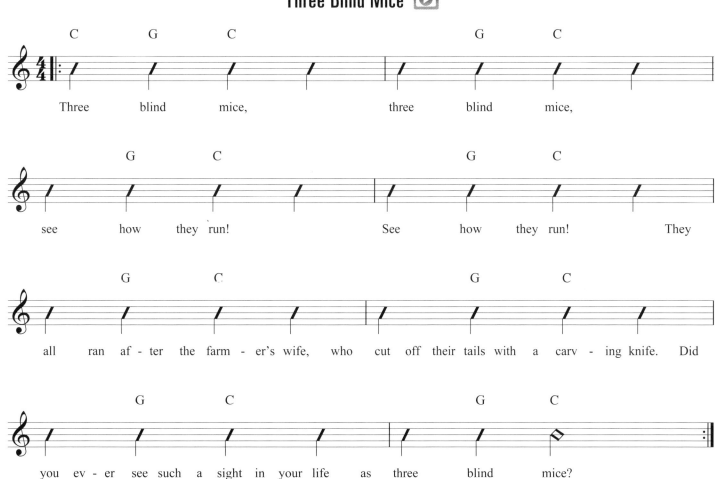

PICKING MELODIES

Now that you've got a start with strumming chords, let's try picking single notes on the Loog. To do this, we're going to use a different kind of notation called *tablature*, or *tab*.

READING TABLATURE

Fretted instruments like the Loog guitar often contain several different places to play the same notes, so the benefit of tablature (indicated at the beginning of a staff with "TAB") is that it tells you exactly where to play each note on the fretboard.

The best way to visualize tablature is to hold your guitar up in front of you, with the lowest-pitched string, the G string (3rd string), closest to the floor. The numbers on the lowest line tell you which frets to play on the G string, the numbers on the middle line tell you which frets to play on the B string, and the numbers on the top line tell you which frets to play on the E string. The number zero (0) tells you to play that string open, or without fretting.

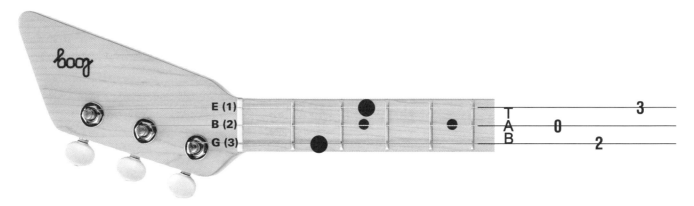

As you read songs in this book, you will see the notes written in the treble clef staff above and the corresponding tablature staff below, like in the exercise on the next page.

3/4 TIME SIGNATURE

So far in this book, you've been playing music with a 4/4 time signature. The top number of a time signature tells you how many beats are in one measure, and the bottom number tells you what note value receives one beat.

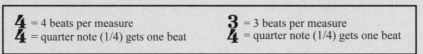

As you can see, the 3/4 time signature is the same as 4/4 except for one important thing: there are *three* beats per measure instead of four.

We begin learning how to pick single notes with the next exercise, "Strum and Pick," because it has a simple quarter-note rhythm (one strum for each beat), and you can play the song with just one finger on the fretboard at a time. This will get you started with moving notes around on the fretboard while still strumming all three strings, as you've been doing with chords. In some sections of the exercise, you will play all open strings, with no fingers on the fretboard.

Play through the exercise first by strumming all three strings for each note, moving the fretted notes as shown in the top staff with the indicated fretting-hand fingerings. Then play it all again, but this time pick only the individual strings, as shown in the tablature. This will require smaller and more precise pick movements since you will be aiming to hit only one string at a time. There are two videos for this exercise so you can hear how both the strummed and picked versions should sound.

Strum and Pick

Strum

Pick

DOTS AND TIES

You might've noticed some new music symbols in the last part of "Strum and Pick." A *dot* that follows a note adds half the value of the note to itself. For example, a *dotted half note* is three beats (2 + 1 = 3) and a *dotted quarter note* is one-and-a-half beats (1 + 1/2 = 1 1/2). A *tie* is a curved line that connects two of the same notes; when two notes are tied, only the first note is picked and is allowed to ring out for the total duration of both notes.

Now try out your note-picking skills with the well-known melody of this classic nursery rhyme. Almost all of the notes are along one string so you can get used to sliding your hand up and down the neck. Use the supplied fretting-hand fingerings and remember to follow the repeat signs.

Mary Had a Little Lamb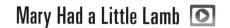

This next song will be more difficult, as the melody notes cross over to different strings. You'll need to slightly adjust your pick hand to move to the different strings smoothly between notes, still picking downward one string at a time.

MUTING

Avoid letting the melody notes ring together. When a note has completed its full duration, release the pressure of your fretting hand to stop it from sustaining before you pick the next melody note. If the note is an open string, then you can *mute* it (stop it from ringing) by touching it lightly with your pick hand, your fretting hand, or both. As you get more experienced with Loog guitar, you'll want to strive for better control over your sound, and muting is a subtle but crucial part of that control.

Aura Lee

EIGHTH NOTES

So far, you've been picking notes and strumming chords using only downward strokes. Now we're going to use the rhythm of the eighth note to learn how to pick and strum both down *and* up.

PICKING EIGHTHS

When picking single notes on the Loog at a fast *tempo* (or speed), we often use alternating downstrokes and upstrokes, in a repeating up-down-up-down cycle. This is called *alternate picking* and is shown in the notation with these symbols:

We count eighth notes with an "and" (&) in between each beat: "1 and 2 and 3 and 4 and"—count them out loud as you play the alternate picking exercise below. Take it slow at first and remember to use small movements with the pick, striking only the B string down and up.

What Goes Up

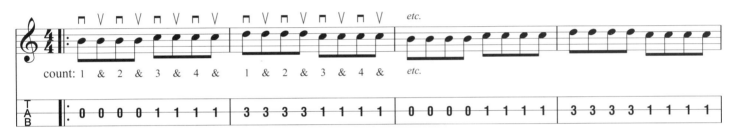

When you feel comfortable playing the exercise at a slow tempo, try it faster. Focus on making each pick stroke even in volume and tone.

LOOG GUITAR APP

Be sure to check out the free Loog Guitar app. You can set your tempo in the Loog app, which features a virtual drummer. It's more fun to play to an actual beat, and it will really help your sense of time.

This simple melody includes eighth notes that you can alternate pick. Your fretting hand will slide back and forth on the neck between the 3rd and 5th frets. Remember to stop the sound of the Loog for the rests.

Hot Cross Buns

STRUMMING EIGHTHS

Just like we can pick single notes with up and down picking, we can do the same with strumming. We use the same notation symbols for downstrums and upstrums. It often helps to say "du" when strumming down and "ah" when strumming up.

This example shows a more complicated rhythm that includes eighth rests. Try speaking the rhythm as shown while you tap your foot at a slow, steady tempo. Then play it on your Loog, strumming just the three open strings.

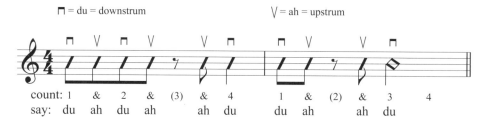

NEW CHORD?

When you strum the three open strings of the Loog, you're playing a chord! It's called the E minor chord and it's often abbreviated like this: Em.

Let's start with a chord strumming exercise that includes the new E minor chord. Follow the strum symbols and strive for a steady, even tone on downstrums *and* upstrums.

Strum Away

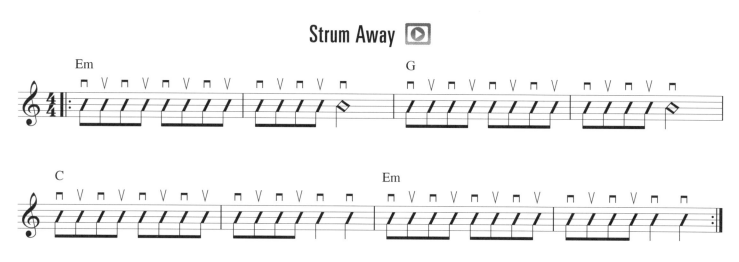

Next, we'll translate our strumming technique to play the melody of "Hot Cross Buns," but this time we'll strum all three strings while we play the melody notes as before. The open strings are not notated in the top staff so you can see the melody notes clearly, but they are shown in the bottom tab staff.

Hot Cross Buns

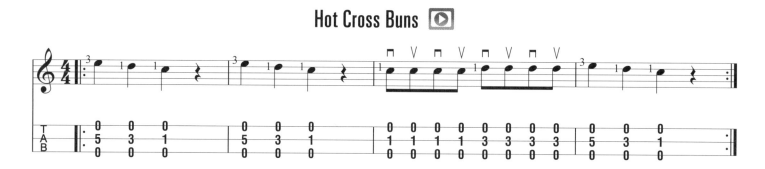

STRUMMING CONCEPTS

When you watch guitarists strumming, you will see that their strumming hand is moving up and down constantly in time to the rhythm of the song. And yet, the sound of the chords is not just a steady eighth-note beat (which would be du–ah–du–ah–du–ah, etc.). We'll call this the "motor-hand technique." While maintaining a steady up-and-down motion with our strumming hand, we will sometimes purposely miss the strings and sometimes mute the strings by releasing pressure on the fretboard. This approach can create a variety of different rhythms and strum patterns to play.

Keep your strumming hand going in a constant up-and-down motion while playing the following two strum patterns. Miss the strings when you see a strum symbol in parentheses, but keep that hand going!

Motor-Hand Strums

Repeat each strum pattern over and over, many times. Try them with different chords, and make up your own strum variations, too!

Let's apply the motor-hand technique to melody playing, similar to what we did with strumming the melody of "Hot Cross Buns." Only the melody notes are shown in the top staff here, but in the motor-hand rhythm you'll be strumming. Notice that you'll need to fret two notes at the same time in measure 4; follow the fretting-hand fingerings.

Mary Motor Hand

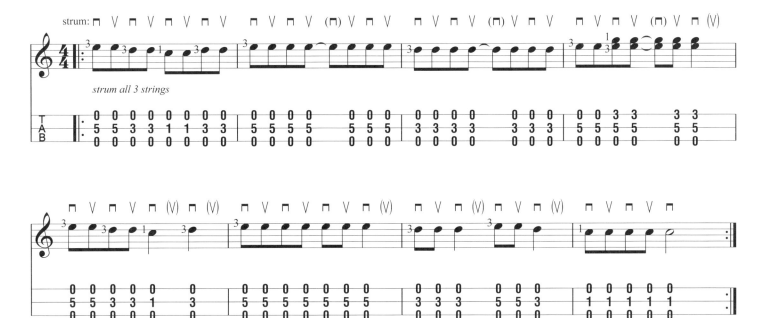

THE F CHORD

So far, you've only been playing *open chords*, which are fretted near the nut of the Loog and include at least one open string. The F chord is your introduction to *barre chords*. These require a different fretting technique in which you hold down multiple notes with only one finger (usually the index). You'll learn more about barre chords later in the book.

For the F chord, you'll need to lay (or *barre*) your index finger across all three strings at the 1st fret. Then, above that finger, put your middle finger on the 2nd fret of the G string. You'll need to clamp your index down pretty firmly to make those notes sound.

SIX-STRING GUITAR

Why should you cover all three strings with your index finger in the F chord? Since your middle finger is fretting the 2nd fret on the G string (above the 1st fret where your index is barring), we technically only need to barre the top two strings of the F chord to play it correctly. However, we cover all three now to get used to the feeling of playing the F chord the way it's played on a standard, six-string guitar, in which you'll need to barre all *six* strings with your index finger. Barring all three strings on the Loog will help increase your hand strength in preparation for six-string guitar, but if you're having too much difficulty with it, you can simply barre only two strings for now.

Get used to playing the F chord with the following strum exercise. It is in 3/4 time, using an eighth-note strum pattern:

F Chord Strum

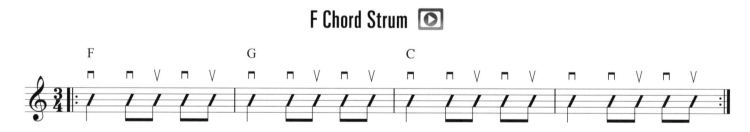

Let's check out the new F chord with a *chord progression*, which is a sequence of chords that repeats within a song. Almost every song you've ever heard contains a chord progression. One basic and popular type of chord progression in blues music is called a *12-bar blues*. It has a 12-bar, or 12-measure, song form. Play it in the next example; the basic slash marks on the staff mean you can strum the chords in any rhythm or pattern you would like.

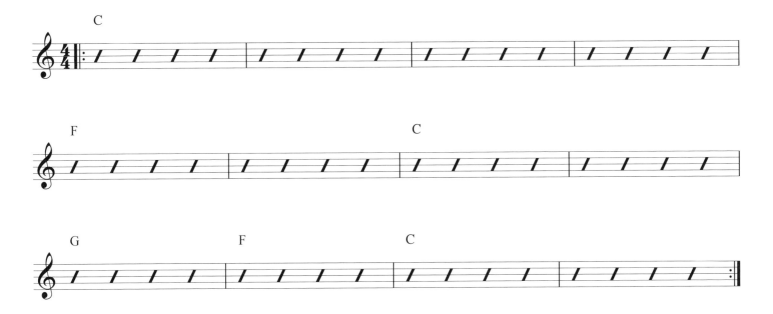

CHORD CHECK

Remember to check your chords to make sure all three notes are ringing clearly. While the chord is fretted, pick each string individually. If any of them are buzzing or producing a dead, muted sound, then you might not be fretting the note with enough pressure, or another finger is touching the string and preventing it from ringing. Identify the problem and adjust your fretting hand until all three notes of the chord are clear.

THE MAJOR SCALE

The next song is in the *key* of C, like many of the tunes you've played so far on the Loog. This means the song centers around the note C, which feels like "home," and includes notes from the C *major scale*:

Note name:	C – D – E – F – G – A – B – C
Scale degree:	1 2 3 4 5 6 7 8 (1)
Chord:	I IV V

We assign each note in the scale a number, or *degree*. The "home" note, or *tonic*, is number 1. Number 8 is also C—just a higher version of that same pitch—one *octave* (or eight notes) higher.

We can also build chords from the scale, and we'll focus on the three *primary chords* that are used in most of the songs in this book: the I, IV, and V chords (Roman numerals are used to represent chords). In the key of C, this would be the C, F, and G chords. Each chord is named after its *root* note from the scale. Check out the table above to see how all of these elements correspond to each other.

ADDING NOTES TO CHORDS

You'll be strumming all three strings throughout "The Sea Waltz" while moving melody notes around within the chords you are fretting. In the chord diagrams below, the solid dots indicate the fretted notes of the chord, and the hollow dots on the fretboard indicate melody notes that are added. The fingerings for the added melody notes are in parentheses. Notice that the fingering for the G chord is different than the way you learned it earlier.

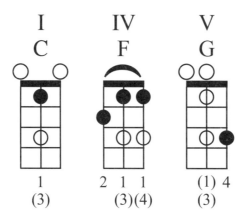

Strum the same 3/4 pattern you played earlier with the F chord. Follow the tab and the provided fingerings. See if you can spot the part of the song that includes the C major scale!

The Sea Waltz ▶

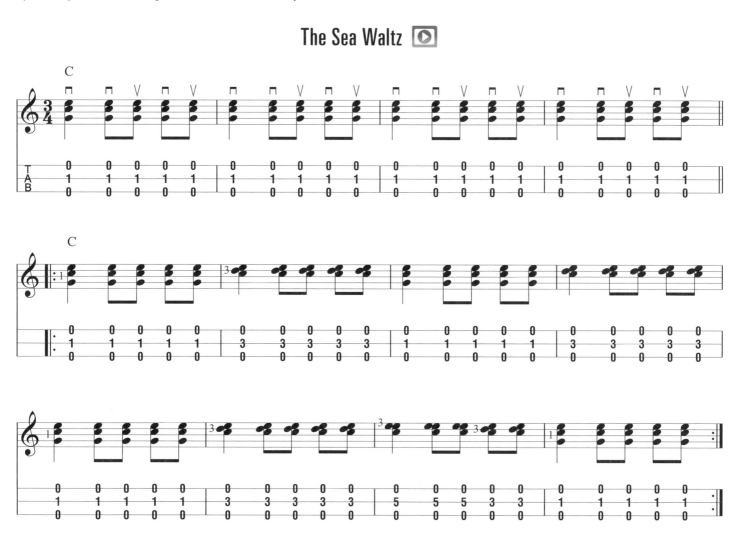

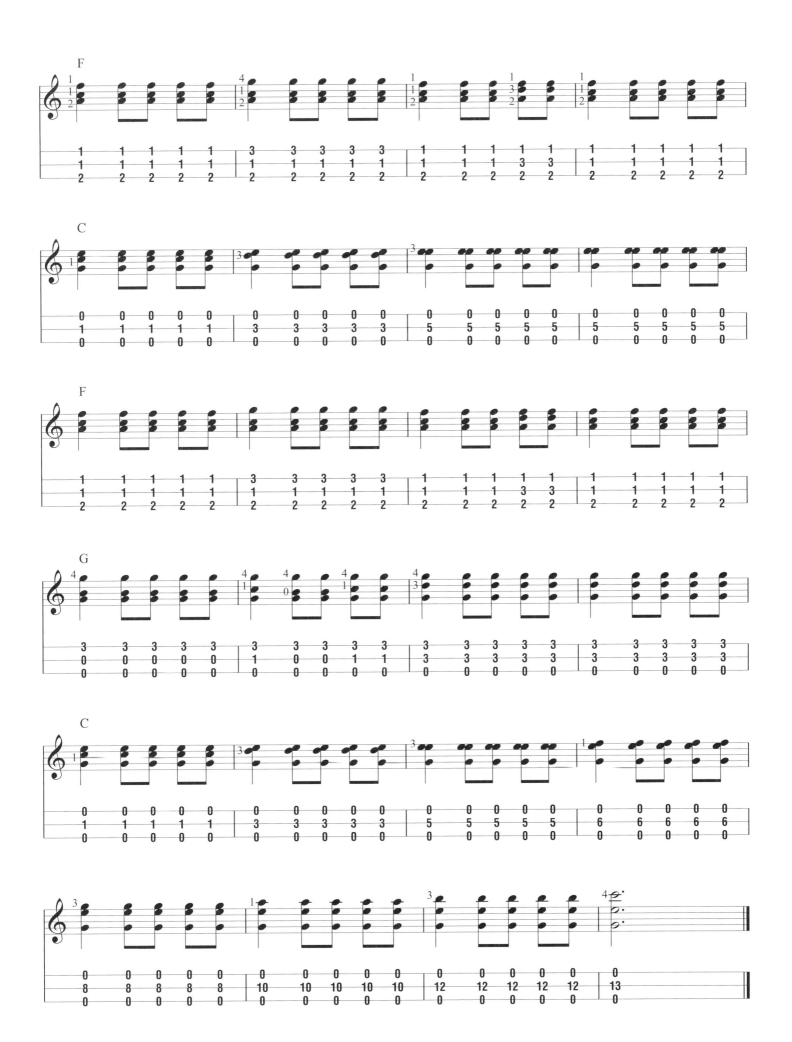

OPEN CHORDS

Let's take a closer look at open chords. We'll start with major and minor *triads*.

Just as there are three wheels on a tricycle, there are three notes in a triad. We refer to those notes as root (R), 3rd (3), and 5th (5). The *root* note determines the letter name of the chord. Here are some examples showing the root, the chord symbol, and the full chord name.

Root Note	Chord Symbol	Chord Name
D	D	D major
A	Am	A minor
G	G	G major

Following, you will see diagrams for some of the most common open chords. They are all played in *1st position*, which basically means the first three frets. In addition to major and minor triads, we have included frequently used *dominant 7th* chords. These are four-note chords that consist of a root, 3rd, 5th, and 7th. To play dominant 7th chords on a three-string Loog guitar, we must leave out the root, 3rd, or 5th.

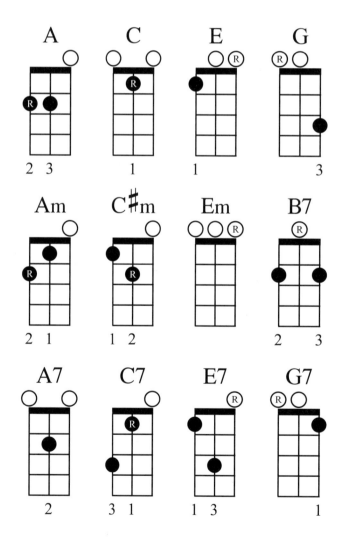

This strum exercise includes many of the new open chords. Follow the strum directions and refer back to the chord diagrams on the previous page if you need help.

Open Chord Strum

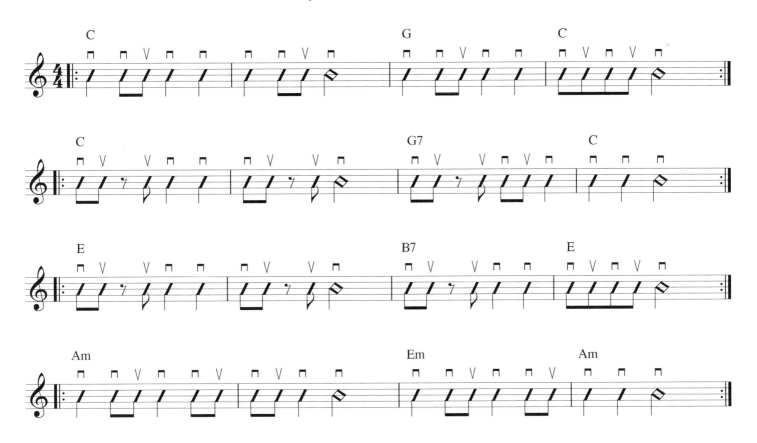

Here are a few more to try out in 3/4 time:

Open Chord Waltz

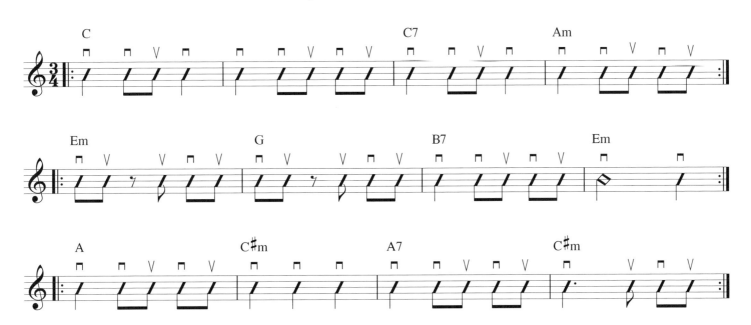

NOTES ON THE NECK

There are only seven letter names for notes in music. Some notes are a *whole step* apart, with a fret in between, and some notes are a *half step* apart, with no fret in between.

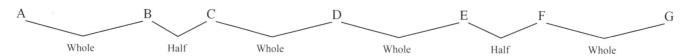

A note with a *sharp* sign (#) after it will be a half step higher in pitch and, therefore, one fret higher on the fretboard. A note with a *flat* sign (♭) after it will be a half step lower in pitch and one fret lower on the fretboard.

To learn all the notes on the fretboard, it is best to play them while saying their names to yourself. Begin by picking the open E string, and then use one finger to fret each note as you move up the neck, one fret at a time, while picking each individual note. Do the same for the B and G strings.

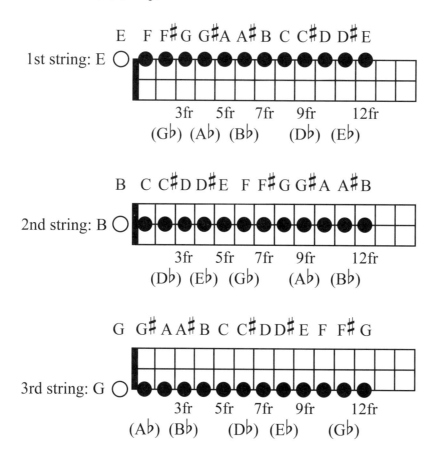

By playing these notes in sequence, you are actually playing a scale—the *chromatic scale*, which includes all 12 possible notes you can play!

ENHARMONICS

Did you notice the flatted notes in parentheses listed underneath the fretboard diagrams above? These are called *enharmonics* and are actually the same notes as their sharped counterparts shown on the fretboards. They are simply a different way to represent the same note.

$$F\# = G♭ \qquad B♭ = A\# \qquad D\# = E♭$$

We used sharps on the fretboard because we were moving up the neck, and likewise, up in pitch. Typically, sharps are used for notes moving up in pitch, and flats are used when they are going down in pitch.

BARRE CHORDS

You were introduced to barre chords with the F chord on page 18. Barre chords are created by laying one finger across two or more strings at the same fret and pressing down to fret the notes. Most of the barre chords in this book are created by laying your 1st finger across all three strings at one fret and filling in the rest of the chord with fingers 2, 3, or 4. On a six-string guitar, it takes a good amount of strength and practice to get every string to ring out on a barre chord. On a three-string Loog guitar, it is much easier, especially for a person with small hands.

There are several advantages to using barre chords rather than open chords:

1. You can *transpose* a song, which means you can play it in a higher or lower key simply by moving the chord shapes up or down the neck.

2. You can create some great rhythms using the motor-hand technique. When you squeeze the neck, you will get the sound of the chord. When you release a little pressure but leave your fretting fingers lightly on the strings, you will get a percussive "chick" sound.

MAJOR BARRE CHORDS

Using the diagrams on the next page, move each chord shape up the neck a half step (one fret) at a time and say the chord names as you go. On the way up the neck, use sharps to name the chords with root notes between the natural notes (A, B, C, D, E, F, G). On the way down, use flats to name these chords. Remember that you are barring across all three strings, and when you release a little pressure, you get a muted "chick" sound.

For this exercise and the following "Minor Barre Workout," use the strum pattern: du *chick*–ah, du *chick*–ah. In other words, let the chord ring for a full quarter note, and with released pressure, strum two muted eighth notes (down–up). The muted strums are shown with an "X" in the notation:

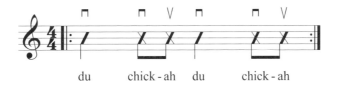

Major Barre Workout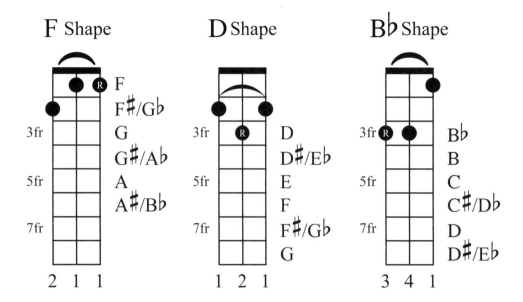

MINOR BARRE CHORDS

As with the major barre chords, move each minor chord shape up the neck a half step at a time and say the chord names as you go. On the way up the neck, use sharps to name the chords with root notes between the natural notes. On the way down, use flats to name these chords.

Use the same strum pattern as before. Remember, let the chord ring for a full quarter note, and with released pressure, strum two muted eighth notes (down–up).

Minor Barre Workout

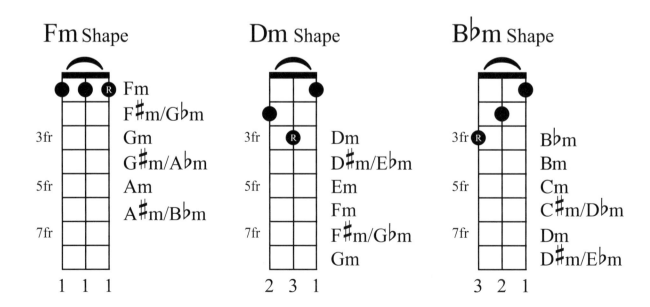

BLUES GROOVES

The 12-bar blues is the foundation of much of American popular music, including jazz and rock. We discussed the blues earlier in the book, and now we'll take a deeper look.

We've also looked at the three primary chords and how those can be derived from the major scale (see page 19). These same primary chords are also the three main chords used in the blues—the I, IV, and V chords. You can figure out the I, IV, and V chords of any key by simply counting up through the letter names. For example, if we are playing a blues in C, C is our I chord ("one chord"). If we go up four steps alphabetically (C–D–E–**F**), we see that F is the IV chord ("four chord"). And if we go up five steps (C–D–E–F–**G)**, we see that G is the V chord ("five chord").

SHUFFLE FEEL

Blues music is often played in a type of rhythmic style called a *shuffle feel* (or *swing feel*). In this style, eighth notes are played with a kind of skipping feel, with the first eighth note in each pair lasting just a bit longer than the second. The shuffle feel has been used in countless songs, so you'll probably recognize it when you hear it. As you work through the following blues tunes, be sure to check out the video to hear and understand the shuffle feel.

Let's revisit the example "12-Bar Blues in C" from earlier in the book, but this time we'll play it using our new barre chord forms instead of open chords. Play the eighth-note rhythms as shown but remember to add the shuffle feel.

12-Barre Blues

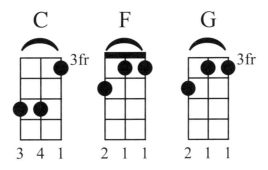

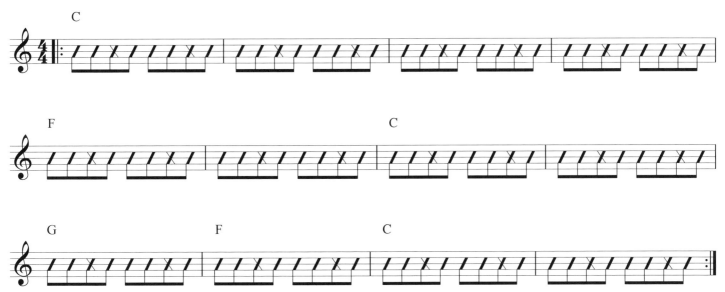

To play the following blues examples and songs, we will use chords with added notes to create *vamps*, or repeating musical patterns. This is a big part of the traditional blues sound.

For this blues in G, there are several new chords to play. Also, in some places (like measure 2), we are changing chords on upstrums (the "ah" part of the beat). This may take a little practice, but eventually you'll be able to do it without even thinking. Play this chord progression with a shuffle feel.

12-Bar Blues in G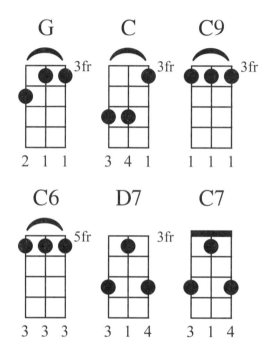

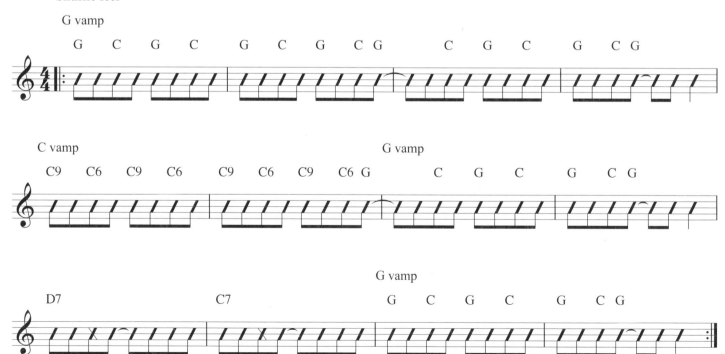

Now, we'll use our G blues vamps and chords from the last example, "12-Bar Blues in G," to play and sing the song "Down to the Dog Pound." On the video, you'll hear two measures of the G vamp as an introduction, and then the first lyric starts right before beat 1 of the first measure.

Down to the Dog Pound ▶

G vamp
Goin' down to the dog pound to find me a brown-eyed pup,

C9 vamp   G vamp
Down to the dog pound to find me a brown-eyed pup,

        D7   C7   G vamp
With a little black nose and a sweet disposition to love.

G vamp
Goin' down to the pet store to find me a singin' bird,

C9 vamp   G vamp
Down to the pet store to find me a singin' bird,

        D7   C7   G vamp
Found a pretty, pretty Polly singin' songs like you never heard.

G vamp
I went to the pawn shop to buy me an old guitar,

C9 vamp   G vamp
Went to the pawn shop to buy me an old guitar,

        D7   C7   G vamp
Found a sweet soundin' baby with a whole lot of miles and heart.

Instead of a shuffle feel, play this E blues with a driving rock feel using the even, or "straight," eighth notes you first learned. There are also several new open chords to try out. Watch out for the quarter rests in measures 5 and 6—remember to mute the strings. This progression will be the accompaniment for the following song, "Dance in the Light of the Sun."

12-Bar Blues in E

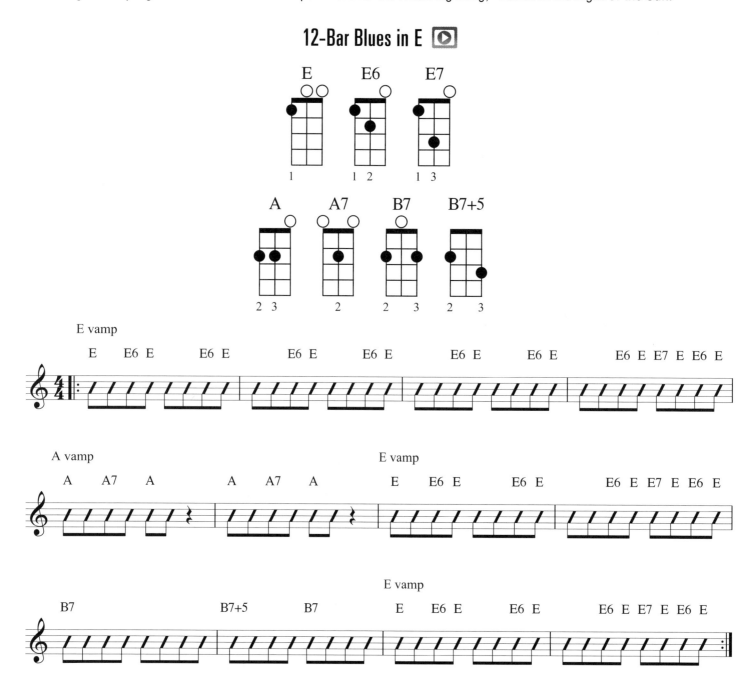

The next song adds lyrics to the "12-Bar Blues in E" you just played. The author wrote the song with a young girl who, after a long stay in the hospital, was going home the next day. When asked what she would do first when she got home, she said, "I'm gonna dance in the light of the sun." On the video, the song begins with an intro of two measures on the E vamp. Notice also there is an interlude guitar solo notated after the lyrics.

Dance in the Light of the Sun

E vamp
I've been waitin' so long for this day to finally come.

A vamp   E vamp
It's been dark but the time is finally done.

B7   B7+5   B7   E vamp
I can't wait to dance in the light of the sun.

Chorus:

E vamp

Dance in the light, dance in the light of the sun.

A vamp   E vamp

Dance in the light, dance in the light of the sun.

B7   B7+5   B7   E vamp

I can't wait to dance in the light of the sun.

E vamp

When I go home, gonna put on my dancin' shoes.

A vamp   E vamp

Nothin' is better for chasin' away the blues.

B7   B7+5   B7   E vamp

When I start dancin', you can dance it too.

Chorus — Interlude — Chorus

Interlude

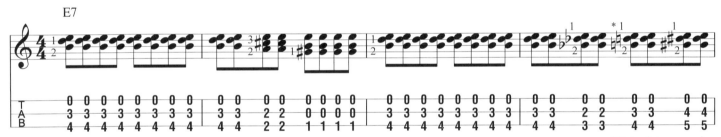

Natural signs cancel
out any previous
sharps or flats on the
same notes in that bar.

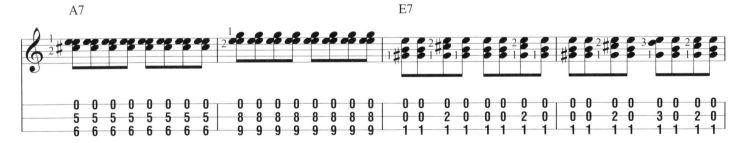

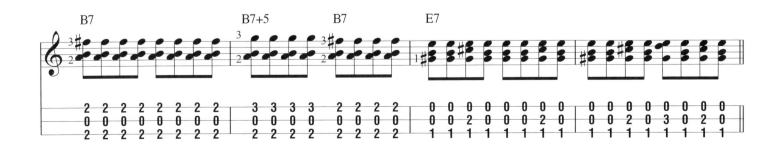

PREPARATION FOR SIX-STRING GUITAR

Playing a Loog guitar is not entirely different from playing standard guitar, it is just simpler. Since we use the same first three strings and tuning as a six-string guitar, everything you learn on a Loog can later be applied to standard guitar. The transition is natural and seamless.

You can use most standard guitar songbooks or song charts to learn to play any song on the Loog guitar. When you see the diagrams for six-string chords, you can ignore the three strings to the left, and play just the three strings to the right.

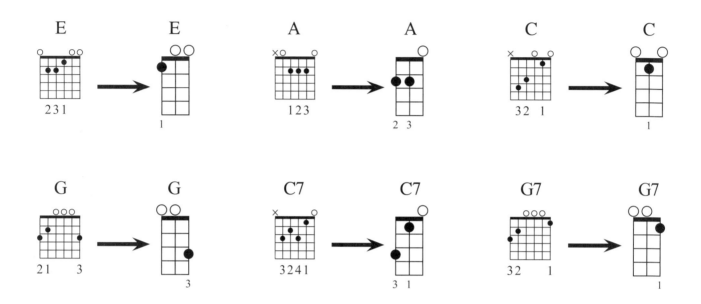

CONCLUSION

Music is a social art. Have fun singing and strumming with friends and family. You should be able to choose any popular song and play it with a Loog guitar accompaniment. Get together with others and write songs of your own.

And for kids, playing a music instrument is beneficial on almost every level: it enhances their cognitive skills, memory, mental processing speed, verbal fluency, creative thinking, and focus. By offering a fun and easy learning experience that allows children to play songs right from Day One, Loog makes kids feel rewarded and encouraged to keep on playing and learning.